First Facts®

MY FIRST GUIDE TO MAGIC TRICKS

by Norm Barnhart and Steve Charney

ROCKFORD PUBLIC LIBRARY

CAPSTONE PRESS
a capstone imprint

First Facts are published by Capstone Press,
1710 Roe Crest Drive, North Mankato, Minnesota 56003
www.capstonepub.com

Library of Congress Cataloging-in-Publication Data
Barnhart, Norm.
  My first guide to magic tricks / by Norm Barnhart and Steve Charney.
     pages cm.—(First facts. My first guides)
  Includes bibliographical references and index.
  Summary: "Step-by-step photo-illustrated instructions show how to perform simple
magic tricks"–Provided by publisher.
  ISBN 978-1-4914-2048-5 (library binding)
  ISBN 978-1-4914-2254-0 (ebook PDF)
1. Magic tricks—Juvenile literature. I. Charney, Steve. II. Title.
  GV1548.B364 2015
  793.8—dc23   2014032618

Editorial Credits
Kathryn Clay and Alesha Sullivan, editors; Tracy McCabe, designer;
Jo Miller, media researcher; Katy LaVigne, production specialist

Photo Credits
All Photos by Capstone Studio: Karon Dubke except: Shutterstock:
Francesco Abrignani, 12 (card face, inset), Olga Dar, cover, 1, 4, 23

Design Elements
Shutterstock: advent, ExpressVectors, LHF Graphics, mhatzapa, MilsiArt

Printed in the United States of America in North Mankato, Minnesota.
092014   008482CGS15

TABLE OF CONTENTS

Full of Surprises

Abracadabra! Have you ever been to a magic show? **Magicians** work in mysterious ways. They entertain and amaze people with their tricks. Becoming a magician doesn't require magic. It just takes a lot of practice! Get started by learning a few simple tricks.

MAGICIAN
a person who performs magic tricks

MAGIC TRICK BASICS

All magicians follow certain rules. Here are the basics to get you started:

1. The most important rule is never to tell anyone how to do a trick. People always ask how the trick is done. But the magician must never share the secret.
2. Another rule is very simple: practice, practice, practice. A magician should be able to do the trick almost without thinking.
3. Try not to do the same trick for the same people. The more often someone sees the trick, the easier it is to figure out how the trick works.
4. Magicians use **patter** to distract the **audience**. The patter keeps the audience's attention. That makes it easier for the magician to do something without anyone seeing.

PATTER
the art of fast talking

AUDIENCE
people who watch or listen to a magic show, movie, or play

No-Pop Balloon

Balloons and pins are usually a poor combination. With a bit of hidden tape, you can amaze your friends with a balloon that won't pop.

MATERIALS

clear tape, a balloon, and two straight pins

GETTING READY:

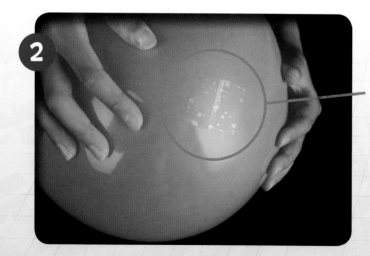

1. Ask an adult to supervise the trick and help you gather the materials.

2. Place two small pieces of tape near the top of a balloon.

THE TRICK:

1. Hold the balloon with the tape toward you so your friend can't see it.

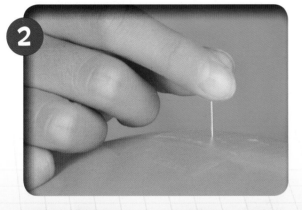

2. One at a time, carefully poke the pins into the tape. The balloon doesn't pop.

3. Take out the pins. Hold one in your hand. To end the trick with a bang, use the pin to pop the balloon. After the trick put the pins away in a container.

Magic Flower Power

Planting flowers is fun. But waiting for the seeds to grow takes a long time. With the help of special seeds, you can make a flower instantly appear.

MATERIALS

a fake flower, a small flower pot, and an empty seed packet

GETTING READY:

1. Place the flower in the flower pot. Hide the flower by holding it against the side of the pot.

THE TRICK:

1. Hold up the pot so the audience can see that it's empty. Be sure to keep the flower hidden under your hand.

2. Tell the audience you have magic seeds. Sprinkle some invisible seeds from the seed packet into the flower pot.

3. Wave your hand over the pot. Reach in and pull out the pretty flower that has magically grown inside!

The "Coolest" Trick

Water usually takes hours to freeze. But magic water instantly becomes ice in this easy trick.

MATERIALS

plastic wrap, a glass of water, a book, and a spoon

GETTING READY:

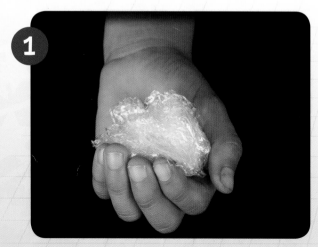

1. Crumple up a piece of plastic wrap. **Palm** it in your left hand.

PALM

to hide something in your hand

THE TRICK:

1. Set a glass of water on the table. Place an open book in front of the glass as shown. Then secretly drop the plastic wrap into the water.

2. Tell your friend that stirring the water will turn it into ice. Stir the water with a spoon. Stirring will unfold the plastic wrap.

3. Say, "Freeze!" Remove the book. The plastic wrap will look like ice in the water.

The Incredible Queen

The Queen of Hearts is the strongest card in a deck. Need proof? Watch as the card holds up a cup on its top edge.

MATERIALS

scissors, an extra playing card, tape, a Queen of Hearts card, and a plastic cup

GETTING READY:

1. First, cut the extra card in half lengthwise.

2. Next, tape one half of the cut card to the back of the Queen card. This creates a secret flap. When the flap is down, the back of the Queen looks like a normal card.

THE TRICK:

1. Hold up the cup and the Queen card. Show the audience both sides of the card. Say, "The card is very strong."

2. Now place the cup on the edge of the card. Secretly bring out the flap to **balance** the cup as shown.

3. Pull your hand away to show that the Queen card is balancing the cup.

BALANCE
to keep steady and not fall

Bottle Bank

A bottle bank is a great place to stash your cash. No need to untwist the cap. Just push the coin right through the side.

MATERIALS

scissors, empty plastic bottle, and a coin

GETTING READY:

1. Ask an adult to help you cut a 1-inch (2.5-centimeter) **slit** near the bottom of a plastic bottle.

SLIT

a narrow cut

14

THE TRICK:

1. Tap the bottom and sides of the bottle with a coin. Show the bottle is whole. Your hand should cover the slit.

2. Unscrew the cap. Show that the bottle is empty.

3. Turn the slit toward you. Tap the coin against the bottle two times. On the third tap, slip it through the slit. Don't let your friend see the slit.

4. Shake the bottle. Turn it upside down. The coin is trapped inside!

An Elephant Every Time

Three animals. One sheet of paper. You'll always pick out the elephant—it's the heaviest one!

MATERIALS

a marker or crayon, a sheet of paper, and a handkerchief

GETTING READY:

1. Draw a ladybug, an elephant, and a cat on the paper as shown. Make sure the elephant is in the middle section. Leave plenty of space between each picture.

16

THE TRICK:

1. First, show the audience the paper with the three pictures. Then tear the paper between the pictures.

2. Turn the pictures upside down. Ask a friend to mix up the pictures. Cover them with the handkerchief while your back is turned.

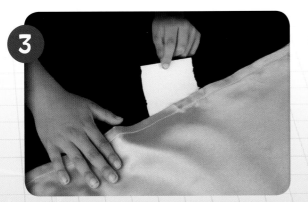

3. Turn back to the table. Say, "I can find the elephant without looking. It is the heaviest one." Then reach under the handkerchief to get the elephant.

4. Pull out the picture of the elephant and take a bow!

The secret to this trick is easy. Simply feel the sides of each piece of paper. The elephant is drawn on the center piece and is the only paper with two torn sides.

The Amazing Olive

Round objects tend to roll away. But magic olives balance nicely on your fingertips.

GETTING READY:

1. Point your index finger up. Secretly hide a toothpick behind your finger. Use your thumb to hold the toothpick in place.

THE TRICK:

1. Say, "I will balance this magic olive on my finger." Pretend to balance the olive as you push the toothpick into the olive.

2. Move your hand as if it's difficult to balance the olive. Keep your palm facing you to hide the toothpick.

3. Remove the olive, and let your friend try. When he or she is not looking, hide the toothpick in your pocket.

Fast Fingers

You have a coin on your elbow. Now it's in your hand. Show off your fast fingers with this speedy trick.

MATERIALS

a coin

THE TRICK:

1. Bend your arm so your hand is next to your ear. Your elbow should point up.

2. Balance a coin on your elbow.

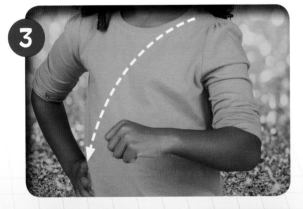

3. Drop your elbow quickly. Your hand will come forward. Grab the coin with your hand as it falls.

4. Show your friend you caught the coin. He or she will be amazed by your speedy skills!

Keep Practicing!

Remember that the secret to doing magic tricks is practice. Now that you know how to do a few simple tricks, keep practicing them. You will soon be able to do these tricks without even thinking about them. Then you'll be ready to become a real magician.

Glossary

audience (AW-dee-uhns)—people who watch or listen to a magic show, movie, or play

balance (BA-luhnts)—to keep steady and not fall

magician (muh-JISH-uhn)—a person who performs magic tricks

palm (PALM)—to hide something in your hand

patter (PAT-uhr)—the art of fast talking

slit (SLIT)—a narrow cut

Read More

Canavan, Thomas. *Magical Illusions*. Miraculous Magic Tricks. New York: Windmill Books, 2014.

Harbo, Christopher L. *Easy Magician Origami*. Easy Origami. North Mankato, Minn.: Capstone Press, 2012.

Hunter, Nick. *Fun Magic Tricks*. Try This At Home!. Chicago: Capstone Raintree, 2013.

Internet Sites

FactHound offers a safe, fun way to find Internet sites related to this book. All of the sites on FactHound have been researched by our staff.

Here's all you do:

Visit *www.facthound.com*

Type in this code: 9781491420485

Check out projects, games and lots more at
www.capstonekids.com